Posttraumatic Stress Disorder: A Guide

Information Centers
Madison Institute of Medicine

This booklet was written by three physicians, John H. Greist, James W. Jefferson, and David J. Katzelnick. The staff of the Madison Institute of Medicine, as always, provided highly relevant literature searches. Susan Heneman improved the clarity of our exposition, and Lynn Tobias and Terese Bailey prepared the numerous drafts of the booklet.

Note: The authors have worked to ensure that all information in this booklet is accurate at the time of publication. As medical research and practice advance, some changes will undoubtedly occur. For this reason, and because human and mechanical errors sometimes occur, we recommend that readers follow the advice of a physician directly involved in their care or in the care of a member of their family.

ISBN # 1-890802-22-0

Contents

Introduction

This booklet is for

People with posttraumatic stress disorder (PTSD)
Families and friends
Anyone interested in learning about PTSD

It is a guide to understanding

What posttraumatic stress disorder is
Treatments used for PTSD
Treatment side effects and how they can be managed
How family and friends can help

We hope it will help

Maximize understanding of posttraumatic stress disorder
Prevent development of PTSD in those who have experienced trauma
Lead to more effective treatment of PTSD
Minimize treatment difficulties
Relieve suffering and restore functioning in people with PTSD

For your reference

A glossary is included beginning on page 59 of this guide

What is posttraumatic stress disorder (PTSD)?

Posttraumatic stress disorder (PTSD) occurs only after exposure to an extremely traumatic experience. After this type of traumatic experience, some people develop symptoms that last a long time. If a person who has experienced an extremely traumatic event develops enough symptoms that last long enough, a diagnosis of posttraumatic stress disorder can be made.

What kinds of events are extremely traumatic? In general, these events involve a direct personal experience of actual or threatened death or serious injury. Sometimes PTSD can result after seeing such an event or learning about the unexpected or violent death, serious harm or threat of death, injury or illness of a loved one.

Not everyone exposed to even the most extreme traumatic events develops PTSD. Those who do develop PTSD often respond to the event with intense fear, helplessness or horror and sometimes with disorganized or agitated behavior. The kinds of events that may produce PTSD include things like "military combat, violent personal assault (sexual assault, physical attack, robbery, mugging), being kidnapped, being taken hostage, terrorist attack, torture, incarceration as a prisoner of war or in a concentration camp, natural or manmade disasters, severe automobile accidents, or being diagnosed with a life threatening illness." Children may develop PTSD after "inappropriate sexual experiences without threatened or actual violence or injury." Witnessing serious injury or unnatural death, or learning about "violent personal assault, serious accident, or serious injury" of a family member or close friend can cause PTSD. PTSD may also result from learning that one's child has a life-threatening illness. When the trauma is caused by a human (such as torture or rape), PTSD may be especially severe or long lasting. In general, the closer one is to the trauma and the more severe the traumatic experience, the greater the likelihood of developing PTSD. The quotes in this paragraph are from the Fourth Edition of the

Diagnostic and Statistical Manual of Mental Disorders (DSM-IV) which was published in 1994. The full section on PTSD is reproduced, with permission, in the Appendix which begins on page 57.

In summary, the traumas that cause PTSD are severe and usually outside the range of common human experience. After such traumatic experiences which would produce a strong reaction in most individuals, some develop an acute stress disorder (see below) and a smaller number progress from acute stress disorder to posttraumatic stress disorder.

Characteristics of acute stress disorder

Three or more of the following are usually present:

1. Numbing, detachment or absence of emotional response
2. Reduced awareness of surroundings (being dazed)
3. Sensation that surroundings are distorted or less real
4. Feeling that one is different, strange or unreal
5. Inability to remember parts of the traumatic experience (amnesia)

In addition to three or more of these five characteristics, the traumatic event is reexperienced repeatedly. Some people have recurrent images, thoughts, dreams, illusions or flashbacks. Others have a sense of reliving the experience or being distressed by reminders of the traumatic event. Further, people avoid reminders of the trauma and experience some of the following symptoms more than they did before the trauma: anxiety, restlessness, difficulty sleeping, irritability, poor concentration, hypervigilance or exaggerated startle response. Taken together, these symptoms cause significant distress or impairment in family, social, work or other important areas of life.

Acute stress disorder begins within four weeks of a trauma and lasts at least two days. If these same symptoms continue more than one month, the diagnosis is changed to acute posttraumatic stress disorder and after three months, PTSD is called chronic. Sometimes PTSD begins many months or years after the trauma. This is referred to as delayed onset PTSD. The formal diagnostic criteria for acute stress disorder and posttraumatic stress disorder are found in the Appendix. The main difference between these disorders is how long each lasts, as seen in Table 1.

Table 1 – Onset and Duration of Traumatic Stress Disorders

	Acute Stress Disorder	Acute PTSD	Chronic PTSD
Onset following trauma	Within 26 days	Immediate or anytime thereafter*	Immediate or anytime thereafter*
Length (Duration)	From 2 days up to 1 month	Up to 3 months	3 months to many years

*includes delayed onset

Experiencing major traumatic events is not rare. In our lifetimes, over half of us will be exposed to the kinds of major traumas that can produce these traumatic stress disorders, but fortunately, far fewer will actually develop them. The best epidemiologic or population studies indicate that about 8% of people living in the United States have had PTSD some time in their lives and that about 5% have PTSD at any particular time. The treatments for PTSD described in this booklet are often very helpful. Unfortunately, most individuals who suffer from PTSD have not sought or received effective treatment. Help is available and most people who get the best treatments will benefit substantially from them.

Common questions about PTSD

What are the symptoms of PTSD? After exposure to an extremely traumatic experience, some individuals reexperience the traumatic event in recollections, flashbacks, nightmares or after encountering reminders of the event. They may also develop emotional numbing and avoid situations that trigger unpleasant memories. Despite emotional numbing, many individuals with PTSD also have increased arousal or alertness. For a diagnosis of posttraumatic stress disorder, all three of these characteristics (reexperiencing, emotional numbing and avoidance, and increased arousal) must be present for more than one month. Let's explore these characteristics in more detail.

Reexperiencing the traumatic event. Most of us remember events, both positive and negative, from our past. Those who suffer PTSD have unwanted, intrusive and distressing recollections of the traumatic event. These range from mildly disturbing memories to flashbacks in which it feels as though the traumatic event is occurring again while the person is awake, or nightmares in which frightening fragments or the entire traumatic event are replayed in dreams. Rarely, at its most extreme level, the person may react both emotionally and physically as though caught up again in the traumatic event.

Emotional numbing and avoidance. Given the unpleasant nature of reexperiencing a traumatic event, there is a certain logic to numbing and avoidance. Unfortunately, the numbing (sometimes called emotional anesthesia) often spreads to involve many important and previously enjoyable activities in addition to those associated with the trauma. Sufferers often describe having a more restricted range of emotions with fewer highs and lows and feelings of detachment from others, including those with whom they had been close before PTSD began. Avoidance may be seen as the ultimate form of numbing.

Increased arousal. Those who have experienced trauma often describe a loss of innocence and trust in their safety and surroundings. They become hypervigilant, watching for danger and often have an exaggerated startle reaction to stimuli that most individuals would hardly notice. Because of increased arousal, individuals with PTSD often have difficulty concentrating and falling or staying asleep and may display irritability because they are always on edge.

As the above description shows, PTSD is a difficult and distressing disorder.

How do I know if I have PTSD? A diagnosis of PTSD is best made by an experienced clinician who understands the signs and symptoms the person is describing in the context of the person's life. Obvious PTSD is easy to recognize but the boundary between PTSD and other psychiatric disorders may be blurred and difficult to define. Some people may seek treatment for relatively mild symptoms; some may avoid treatment even when they have severe PTSD; still others may have another disorder that needs to be sorted out from PTSD. You might find the following checklist helpful. Check **yes** or **no** after reading each question.

A checklist of signs and symptoms of PTSD:

Criterion A: The trauma

Yes ___ No ___ 1. Have you felt intense fear, helplessness or horror as a result of experiencing, witnessing or learning about a life threatening event?

Criterion B: Reexperiencing the trauma

Are you having any of the following:

Yes ___ No ___ 1. Unwanted intrusive and distressing recollections of the event?

Yes ___ No ___ 2. Flashbacks (while awake feeling as if the event is occurring again)?

Yes ___ No ___ 3. Nightmares of the event or parts of the event?

Yes ___ No ___ 4. Feeling or acting as though you are experiencing the event when you are reminded of the event?

Criterion C: Emotional numbing and avoidance

Have any of the following begun since the traumatic experience?

Yes ___ No ___ 1. Efforts to avoid thoughts, feelings or conversations associated with the trauma?

Yes ___ No ___ 2. Efforts to avoid activities, places or people that arouse recollections of the trauma?

Yes ___ No ___ 3. An inability to recall an important aspect of the trauma?

Yes ___ No ___ 4. A markedly diminished interest or participation in significant activities?

Yes ___ No ___ 5. A feeling of detachment or estrangement from others?

Yes ___ No ___ 6. A restricted range of affect (e.g., unable to have loving feelings)?

Yes ___ No ___ 7. A sense of a foreshortened future (e.g., does not expect to have a career, marriage, children or a normal life span)?

*Both avoidance and numbing must be present (at least one symptom from C1-3 and at least one from C4-7) with a total of three symptoms from C1-7.

Criterion D: Increased arousal

Since the trauma, have you noticed any of these changes in yourself?

Yes ___ No ___ 1. Excessive wariness or vigilance?

Yes ___ No ___ 2. Exaggerated startle response?

Yes ___ No ___ 3. Difficulty concentrating?

Yes ___ No ___ 4. Difficulty sleeping?

Yes ___ No ___ 5. Increased irritability?

Please remember that the results you get from completing the checklist are not diagnostic. Your doctor can help you put them in context. As a rough guide to the possibility of a PTSD diagnosis, look back over your answers. In addition to answering **yes** to the trauma question (Criterion A), you must have at least one yes answer in the reexperiencing category and three avoidance and emotional numbing symptoms. Two increased arousal symptoms must also be present. The full DSM-IV criteria used to make a formal diagnosis of PTSD are listed in the Appendix beginning on page 57.

What causes PTSD? PTSD is always caused by a trauma that most people would recognize as extremely distressing. The more severe the trauma and the longer a person is exposed to it, the greater the likelihood of developing PTSD. If the trauma is caused by human action, the likelihood of PTSD is also increased. Thus, kidnapping followed by torture would be more likely to cause PTSD than a storm damaging your house. Fortunately, PTSD does not occur in everyone exposed to severe trauma. On the other hand, some individuals develop PTSD after exposure to relatively minor trauma. Why some people develop PTSD after a seemingly minor trauma is unknown. Young age, exposure to previous traumas (including childhood sexual abuse) and possibly the presence of other mental disorders may predispose a person to PTSD.

How common is PTSD? Different studies have found somewhat different levels of PTSD. However, most studies have found PTSD to be more common than previously recognized. The National Comorbidity Survey, conducted with more than 8,000 citizens selected to represent the United States population, found an 8% lifetime rate of PTSD and identified that 5% of Americans currently suffer from PTSD. The difference between lifetime and current rates means that some who experience PTSD recover from it.

Does PTSD occur in children and the elderly? PTSD can affect people of any age. People of all ages are exposed to extreme traumas which are at least upsetting. Children may be more vulnerable to developing PTSD, perhaps because they have had less life experience and less naturalistic exposure therapy after traumatic events. Conversely, elderly individuals may have emergence or reemergence of PTSD as brain function declines with age. Some veterans of World War II and Korean combat are experiencing PTSD for the first time, perhaps because their aging brains have lost some of the natural defense mechanisms that previously protected them from PTSD.

After traumatic experiences, what can be done to prevent PTSD from developing? One important way to prevent PTSD is to confront traumatic memories rather than trying to suppress or avoid them. Exposing oneself to the traumatic memories causes short-term distress but as a process known as habituation has time to work, the traumatic memories usually lose their sting. Avoiding these memories often helps them solidify at a somewhat less conscious level and leads to reexperiencing phenomena outside the individual's control. Poet Alfred Lord Tennyson had it right: "Face the thing you fear the most and it will be the certain death of it."

Treatment of PTSD

Although many who suffer traumas and later develop posttraumatic stress disorder recover without treatment, others go on to have chronic posttraumatic stress disorder that interferes with daily life and causes great distress. Those with PTSD often develop other disorders, perhaps as a consequence of their PTSD. For example, some with PTSD turn to alcohol or other drugs. Depression or anxiety disorders such as social anxiety disorder, panic disorder or obsessive compulsive disorder may also occur. After PTSD begins, it often feeds on itself and progresses to the point of becoming a severe disability. Treating PTSD can lessen distress and restore functioning. Certain psychotherapies and medications can be effective treatments for PTSD even after it has become chronic.

Importantly, some PTSD can be prevented if individuals who have been traumatized do the right things after the trauma. While it is understandable that well-intentioned friends, family and even clinicians might advise staying away from the traumatic scene, reminders of the trauma or even thoughts of the trauma ("Just try not to think about it"), these suggestions are **wrong**. It has been conclusively established through military and civilian experience that distancing the victim of a trauma from reminders and memories of the trauma increases rather than decreases the risk of developing posttraumatic stress disorder.

Medical policy in modern armies advocates removing the soldier with acute stress disorder (sometimes called shell shock or battle fatigue) only a short distance from the scene of battle and for only a short time. Although the soldier may appear largely unable to function when he reaches the aid station, he is not evacuated to the rear area. Instead, he is told that the experience he has been through is frightening, traumatizing and, as he perceived, life threatening. Ideally, he will also be given dry clothing, a warm place to sleep and hot rations, and ordered to help in the aid station activities. In short, he's given an accurate explanation for what he is experiencing, a brief rest and then returned to his unit where his comrades need and support him. Most soldiers treated in this way recover rapidly and do not develop posttraumatic stress disorder. The old saying "get back on the horse that threw you" is the civilian equivalent of the military management of acute stress disorder. Preventing a disorder is always a better policy than treating it after it becomes a problem.

Psychotherapies for PTSD

Three kinds of psychotherapy have been shown through careful research to be effective treatments for PTSD. At this stage in our knowledge and understanding, it is impossible to say which of these treatments, alone or in combination, will be most helpful for a given individual. Exposure therapy, anxiety management and cognitive therapy all have advocates, but the wise therapist will offer all three and emphasize the one(s) that proves most helpful for each patient. It is ideal to work with a therapist experienced in treating PTSD with these therapies of proven effectiveness. Unfortunately, such therapists are few and they are in great demand.

The descriptions of psychotherapies that follow are intended as guides to the important elements of effective therapies. They are not a substitute for a skilled therapist but may be helpful to some who cannot find or afford a therapist.

Exposure therapy

Exposure therapy is based on the principle that we get used to things that are just annoying and not truly dangerous. This is called habituation and it occurs naturally in over 95% of people. Exposure therapy recognizes that habituation must occur in the person who has been traumatized. While a therapist may be useful as a guide, habituation occurs within the patient—not in the relationship between patient and therapist.

For example, visiting a friend in a large city who lives in a second floor apartment just beside an elevated railroad would seem very annoying every time a train screeched by, shaking the building and rattling the windows to the point that conversation became difficult. One might even say to the friend, "How do you live in this din?" The friend might answer, "What din?" If we only visit, we leave with a belief that our friend lives in an impossible situation; if we stay in the apartment for a week or two, we are no longer annoyed by passing trains and may not even be aware of them.

Exposure therapy is the opposite of the usual approach of avoidance. Many people want to avoid the triggers of their discomfort. Avoidance may provide temporary relief, but that relief doesn't last. The triggers must be faced to get the benefits of fewer and milder PTSD symptoms.

Exposure therapy asks patients to confront, in a safe way, the very situations, objects, people and memories attached to the trauma. Before therapy these triggers continue to produce grossly unrealistic fears long after the trauma or risks of repeated trauma have ended.

Exposure may be done in vivo (in real life) or in imagination. In vivo exposure is more effective than imaginal exposure. Although anxiety or other discomfort may get worse in the first minutes of exposure, if the exposure is continued long enough, habituation occurs and anxiety fades. It is important to continue exposure until discomfort has diminished because escaping the discomfort reinforces avoidance as a coping tactic and produces all the limitations associated with avoidance. Put another way, when a person avoids triggers of anxiety, he may avoid that anxiety. But he buys that comfort at the price of not being able to go to the places he avoids. Avoidance also encourages a spread of anxiety, first to similar anxiety triggers and often to triggers that have little, if anything, to do with the original anxiety. Repeated exposure reinforces mastery of anxiety through habituation and empowers the individual rather than weakening him through avoidance. Examples of exposure in vivo are resuming driving after being in a traumatizing accident; returning to a site, now safe, where an assault occurred; and no longer avoiding settings that remind the person of the trauma.

Exposure in imagination involves the person recounting traumatic memories until they lose their sting. This can be done by saying them aloud repeatedly, writing, reading and rewriting a biography of the events, or recording them on a tape and playing them over and over until they are no longer distressing.

Anxiety management

Anxiety management involves learning several skills to help you cope better with PTSD symptoms. People usually try all of these anxiety management techniques to determine which one(s) helps most. Then, when PTSD symptoms are troublesome, the anxiety management techniques are used to reduce distress and intensity of the symptoms. Once again, these techniques should be learned and practiced until they are easy to carry out when distress occurs. It is not enough to understand the principles behind these techniques; they must be practiced repeatedly until they can be employed easily and automatically, almost without thinking about them. Five different techniques for anxiety management are: breathing retraining, relaxation, assertiveness training, positive thinking and self-talk, and thought stopping.

Breathing retraining

When we feel frightened or anxious, a natural part of our "fight or flight" response is to breathe more rapidly and deeply. Many times we are unaware of this increase in breathing and if it is pronounced and exceeds our body's need for increased oxygen and clearing of carbon dioxide, it is called hyperventilation. Hyperventilation can produce uncomfortable or even frightening sensations that make you feel more anxious. In fact, some describe a "vicious cycle" in which anxiety or fear provokes hyperventilation which, in turn, worsens the anxiety or fear. Symptoms of hyperventilation often include a sensation of shortness of breath. Other hyperventilation symptoms are lightheadedness or dizziness, chest tightness, trembling, "pins and needles" sensations, usually in the fingers, toes or scalp, and nausea or other stomach problems. Different people experience different symptoms.

Hyperventilation almost always involves rapid and/or deep breathing using chest muscles to expand the rib cage. Some are able to return their breathing to a normal rate and volume by repeating something like "slow and shallow" and systematically breathing once every 4 or 5 seconds (12 to 15 times a minute). Others prefer to learn and practice the technique of abdominal or belly breathing. One way to rehearse this technique is to lie on the floor on your back and breathe by moving your abdomen out when you breathe in, and in when you breathe out, while trying to use your chest muscles and rib cage as little as possible. Putting a book on your abdomen may help you get it right. Once again, keeping the rate of breathing at 12 to 15 breaths a minute is important.

Relaxation

When frightened or anxious, we tighten our muscles so that we are ready to fight, flee or freeze. While this reaction is appropriate in the face of imminent danger, PTSD symptoms are a reaction to past danger and inappropriate in the present.

There are a number of relaxation techniques. More than 60 years ago, Edmund Jacobson devised an easily learned technique. First you contract and then relax large muscle groups. Do this repeatedly in one part of the body to increase your awareness and control of the process of tensing and relaxing muscles. For example, tense your right forearm and fist, holding the tension until it is uncomfortable and then consciously say the word, "relax" while relaxing your fist and forearm. You become aware of the discomfort associated with tense muscles. As tension occurs in response to PTSD triggers, you can first consciously, and later less consciously, relax muscles that are becoming tense. Simply sitting in a relaxed position, closing your eyes, and saying a neutral word such as "one," or other approaches you may find in popular self-help programs may also be helpful. No one of them is necessarily better than another but one may work better for you.

Assertiveness training

Assertive communication is the direct and honest expression of your feelings, preferences, needs or opinions in a way that does not offend or threaten another person. It means standing up for your legitimate rights without violating the rights of others and telling people what you feel or want, directly and honestly, without stepping on their toes. Unassertive communication occurs when you do not directly express your feelings, needs or opinions.

Many people have fallen into a pattern of unassertive communication and for those with PTSD, this pattern often accentuates their distress and dysfunction. By observing your pattern of communication and how you feel when communicating, you can assess how assertive you are in expressing your feelings, needs or opinions.

You can tell the difference between being aggressive, passive or appropriately assertive. Aggressive communication comes across as too strong and violates the rights of others. Passive communication comes across as too weak and doesn't express directly what you really want to say. Assertive communication comes across as direct, clear, brief and honest. Getting more comfortable with assertive communication takes practice. Assertive communication can be hard for many of us in the following situations:

1. Expressing our positive feelings
2. Expressing our negative feelings honestly and politely
3. Standing up for our rights in a relationship or situation
4. Accepting a compliment

Here are some tips about assertive communication. Ask yourself the following four questions and notice your responses. You may want to write them on a card and carry them with you for easy reference.

1. **How anxious or relaxed was I?**
   Did I look the person in the eye?
   Was my posture relaxed?
   Did the distance between us feel right?
   Did I make many unnecessary body movements?

2. **What did I say?**
   Did I decide what my goals were *before* I said anything?
   Did I say what I really wanted to say?
   Was I concise and to the point?
   Was I definite, specific and firm?

3. **How did I say it?**
   Did I avoid explanations, excuses or apologies?
   Did I start with "I feel...." when appropriate?
   Did I ask for advice about what to say in a tough situation?

4. **And?**
   Did I talk right after the other person stopped?
   Was there hesitancy or stammering in my voice?
   Was my volume, tone and inflection appropriate?
   Did I avoid whining, pleading or accusing?

Positive thinking and self-talk

Here the goal is to replace negative or destructive thoughts with positive or constructive thinking. For example, instead of thinking, "I can never control my emotions," we can learn to think and even say to ourselves, "No one can control all their emotions all the time, but is it really true that I can never control my emotions? No. I can think about times when I have had better control over my emotions." Here are some questions you can ask yourself about your thinking:

1. Am I thinking negative thoughts that bring me down or interfere with reaching my goals?
2. Do I criticize myself instead of encouraging and rewarding myself?
3. Do I think negatively about myself, my situation or my future?
4. Am I focusing on negative things and excluding positive things in my life?
5. Can I help myself feel better by changing what I say to myself?
6. What positive thought do I want to focus on?
7. What other viewpoints are there?
8. How else can I view this so I am being more neutral?
9. Is it really as bad as I think?
10. What is the evidence for this thought?
11. How true is this thought?
12. Am I focusing just on the negative and not recognizing the positives in myself or my situation?
13. Am I thinking in all-or-nothing terms or using "should" statements that upset me?
14. Am I predicting the future instead of experimenting with it?

One popular book that provides details about constructive thinking is *Feeling Good* by David Burns (see Suggested Readings on page 53).

Thought stopping

Thought stopping asks you to stop thoughts that are distressing. Often a therapist asks the person to think a distressing thought and when the person indicates that the thought is clearly in mind, the therapist shouts, "Stop." This startles the person and interrupts the thought. The person is then taught to first shout, later say and finally whisper, "Stop" whenever a distressing thought occurs.

This anxiety management technique is controversial because it is the opposite of what exposure therapy requires. Exposure therapy, which has been shown to be very effective in treating PTSD, requires long periods of confronting the triggers of PTSD discomfort to permit habituation to occur. Thought stopping, by contrast, maintains that one should stop or turn off discomforting thoughts. While this may provide short-term relief for some individuals, it seldom provides lasting benefit as the distressing thoughts and feelings and behaviors that accompany the thoughts almost always come back. Most people with PTSD have tried to stop their thinking or distract themselves from their thoughts many times without finding this approach helpful. In fact, thought stopping before habituation has time to work may make the person more sensitive to the very thoughts being stopped. So, you can see why thought stopping is controversial. If it seems very helpful for you, you might hold it in reserve for specific instances when other anxiety management techniques are difficult to employ. Don't be surprised or disappointed if thought stopping proves ineffective. Just leave it alone and use other anxiety management techniques that work better for you.

Cognitive therapy

Cognitive therapy is very much like the positive or constructive thinking discussed above under anxiety management. The goals of cognitive therapy are to:

1. Show how your thoughts affect your feelings
2. Help you spot self-defeating, negative thoughts that cause distress
3. Help you change negative thoughts to more positive ones

There are four steps to reducing negative thinking:

1. Become more aware of thoughts that distress you
2. Pay attention to the connections among your thoughts, feelings and behaviors
3. Challenge (talk back to) your negative thoughts
4. Substitute positive thoughts for negative ones

Information and education

Learning about PTSD is very important. This booklet provides a lot of information about PTSD but is by no means comprehensive. Many other fine books are available (see Suggested Readings, page 53). This booklet was prepared by doctors who have treated patients with posttraumatic stress disorder and reflects their review of the scientific literature as well as their clinical experience. Expert Consensus Panels on PTSD provided data from which guidelines were developed and published as Supplement 16, Volume 60, 1999 of the *Journal of Clinical Psychiatry* (see Suggested Readings–Technical on page 54). Copies of these guidelines can be obtained (for the cost of $10.00) from the publishers at Physicians Postgraduate Press, Inc., P.O. Box 752870, Memphis, TN 38175-2870, telephone 1-800-489-1001, extension 114. You can also download the guidelines from the web site www.psychguides.com.

Supportive counseling

All patients need and deserve support and empathetic understanding. Supportive psychotherapy helps by shoring up defenses, utilizing strengths, empathizing with distress, explaining the characteristics and course of PTSD, monitoring changes and reassuring the patient that improvement will, in time, occur. With the patient's permission, support and explanation should also be provided to family members, friends and others important in the patient's life. These individuals constitute a network of support more accessible than anything the doctor can provide. When other treatments are ineffective, support by caring others can sustain a person until PTSD resolves on its own with the passage of time as it sometimes does. Family doctors often know patients best and are, therefore, a most important source of information and support.

Support groups for those with PTSD are often available. The Anxiety Disorders Association of America (see Resources on page 55) has listings of many self-help groups in the United States.

For those with access to the Internet, several web sites are recommended beginning on page 55. Remember that the World Wide Web contains information of widely variable quality, leading one wag to call it the world *wild* web.

Play therapy

Young children are seldom able to discuss events and their emotions about them as fully as adults. Play therapy permits indirect or symbolic expressions of emotion and events and is sometimes used to help children in the process of recovery from traumas they have experienced. Play therapy may be viewed as a form of exposure therapy for children.

Other psychotherapies

Psychodynamic psychotherapy derived from psychoanalytic theory and therapy was the most widely practiced form of psychotherapy for many decades. Its theories are very appealing and some practitioners still emphasize them, although the evidence for benefit from psychodynamic psychotherapy for PTSD is slim, at best. Still, when people develop PTSD, their beliefs about security and predictability of the world are shaken. This understandable loss of innocence is dispiriting and leads to great soul searching. It is as though PTSD sufferers are grieving their loss of innocence about the sometimes cruel realities of life. While work and the passage of time is a powerful antidote for sorrow, some may benefit from psychotherapy focused on the unpredictability of life and the inability to guarantee safety. The goal of such psychotherapy is to help the individual regain a balanced perspective on the risks we all face.

It is understandable that sufferers of PTSD would want to have their repeated recall and reexperiencing of the trauma stopped. Hypnotherapists seem to offer the possibility of erasing these unpleasant recollections. Finally, a new therapy called eye movement desensitization reprocessing (EMDR) has had some positive results although most studies have found EMDR to be ineffective. When effective, it may be that EMDR is a form of exposure therapy as it asks people to hold the traumatic event in consciousness while moving their eyes in a particular manner. The Expert Consensus Panels were asked about "eye movement desensitization reprocessing (EMDR), hypnotherapy, and psychodynamic psychotherapy, but they did not rate these techniques highly for the treatment of PTSD." (Expert Consensus Guidelines, page 14).

Medications for PTSD

Many have felt that medications have little to offer PTSD sufferers. This is no longer true. Unfortunately, many people still believe medications are of little value and some who write about PTSD still express these mistaken beliefs, ignoring the sound research on which use of medications is based.

Certain medications have now been shown to be effective treatment for PTSD. As of May, 2000, the U.S. Food and Drug Administration (FDA) has approved one medication, sertraline (Zoloft), for treating PTSD. Other medications in the same selective serotonin reuptake inhibitor (SSRI) class as sertraline are probably effective. Based on the research evidence, the Expert Consensus Panels recommend an SSRI as the best first-line treatment for PTSD. The five SSRIs available in the United States are:

citalopram (Celexa)
fluoxetine (Prozac)
fluvoxamine (Luvox)
paroxetine (Paxil)
sertraline (Zoloft) – FDA approved indication for PTSD

In addition to proven effectiveness, the SSRIs are preferred over older medications because their side effects are fewer and less troubling. If one SSRI is ineffective or has intolerable side effects, a second SSRI may prove beneficial and be well tolerated.

The Expert Consensus Panels also saw promise in two comparatively new antidepressants, nefazodone (Serzone) and venlafaxine (Effexor), and more recent data suggest that the same can be said for bupropion (Wellbutrin) and mirtazapine (Remeron). Because of their more favorable side effect profiles, their use should be considered ahead of tricyclic antidepressants.

Two older tricyclic antidepressants (imipramine [Tofranil] and amitriptyline [Elavil]) have also shown benefit in research trials and have been used in the treatment of PTSD. Tricyclic antidepressants are not preferred treatments, primarily because of their more frequent and troublesome side effects.

We are sure you've noticed by now that we have been describing antidepressants as a treatment for PTSD, an anxiety disorder. Many medications achieve initial approvals from the FDA for one indication (in this case depression) and are later found to be helpful for other disorders. This is certainly true for the SSRIs. In addition to FDA approvals for depression, different members of the SSRI class also have FDA approvals for bulimia, panic disorder, posttraumatic stress disorder, premenstrual dysphoric disorder (approval pending as of June, 2000), obsessive-compulsive disorder (fluvoxamine is FDA-approved for only this indication) and social anxiety disorder. SSRIs are broad spectrum psychopharmacologic agents and the initial FDA labeling for depression should not concern you if they are prescribed for other indications. Physicians often prescribe medications "off label" when they are found to be helpful for a particular condition even if they have not been approved for that use by the FDA. These "antidepressants" are also effective treatments for PTSD in much the same way aspirin treats fever and inflammation as well as pain for which it is most often used.

Antianxiety medications (anxiolytics) include benzodiazepines such as alprazolam (Xanax), clonazepam (Klonopin), diazepam (Valium) and lorazepam (Ativan), as well as the non-benzodiazepine buspirone (BuSpar). The benzodiazepines have the merit of reducing anxiety rapidly, often within hours, but may have counterbalancing side effects early in the course of their use that include sedation and incoordination, and the development of physical dependency in those who use them for more than a few weeks. Buspirone does not cause significant physical dependency but seldom alleviates anxiety before one, two or more weeks have passed. Benzodiazepines and buspirone have not been shown to be effective treatments for PTSD when used alone. As adjunctive (add-on) medication they may be helpful.

The Expert Consensus Panels also recognized a role for mood stabilizers such as divalproex (Depakote) as augmentation (add-on) if there has been a poor response to an antidepressant alone. They may be particularly helpful for those who have lots of irritability, anger or hostility. Mood stabilizers (lithium [Eskalith, Lithobid and others], carbamazepine [Carbatrol, Tegretol], gabapentin [Neurontin], lamotrigine [Lamictal] and topiramate [Topamax] in addition to divalproex) are used to treat bipolar (manic-depressive) disorder so that those with that disorder in addition to PTSD would almost certainly receive a mood stabilizer as part of their treatment.

A class of medications called monoamine oxidase inhibitors (MAOIs) has also been shown to be helpful in PTSD. However, MAOIs are rarely used because of more frequent side effects than found with SSRIs and because a careful diet must be followed to prevent dangerous increases in blood pressure.

In summary, SSRIs have the strongest evidence for efficacy and tolerability as treatments for PTSD, and sertraline (Zoloft) has received FDA approval for this indication. SSRIs are first-line medication treatment for PTSD. Nefazodone (Serzone) and venlafaxine (Effexor), and possibly bupropion (Wellbutrin) and mirtazapine (Remeron), are second-line treatments if SSRIs prove ineffective or are not well tolerated. Tricyclic antidepressants would be employed if the person has had a good response to them in the past and they do not cause severe side effects or if the person has failed to respond to or does not tolerate SSRIs, nefazodone, venlafaxine, bupropion or mirtazapine. MAOIs would usually be used when they have been effective in earlier treatment or when the other classes of antidepressants have not been helpful. Mood stabilizers may be added to improve a partial response to an antidepressant while antianxiety benzodiazepines would ideally be used only briefly and intermittently to quell acute and severe anxiety symptoms. Buspirone may be a helpful adjunctive treatment for anxiety symptoms in people with PTSD although evidence for its effectiveness is limited.

If a medication is well tolerated, most patients should continue to take it for 6 to 12 months if they have acute PTSD (less than 3 months duration) and for at least 12 and as long as 24 months for chronic PTSD before trying to taper off the medication. If PTSD symptoms return when medication is being tapered for discontinuation, the effective dose would be resumed and usually continued for an even longer time before discontinuation is tried again.

Beginning medication therapy for PTSD

What will your doctor need to know before prescribing medication for PTSD?

Your medical history—Do you have other medical conditions? For example, you may be asked about heart disease, thyroid problems and other endocrine (hormone) disorders, epilepsy and other disorders of the nervous system, liver disease, etc. Some medical illnesses may worsen or even cause PTSD-like symptoms. **Any medical condition** you have may be important, so be sure to give the doctor a complete listing. Is there any history of psychiatric illness in your family, especially posttraumatic stress disorder, depression, mania or alcohol abuse?

Any medications you are taking—For example, are you taking medications such as antihypertensives (for lowering blood pressure), benzodiazepines (for anxiety or sleep), barbiturates (sleeping pills), antiparkinson drugs, steroids or antipsychotics? **Any medication** you are taking may be important, so be sure to inform your doctor of **all medications** (including nonprescription drugs and herbal products). Some medications may worsen or even cause PTSD-like symptoms and some may interact adversely with the medicine your doctor will prescribe. Also, you will be asked if you have ever had an allergic reaction or an intolerance to an antidepressant or any other medicine.

Your occupation and activities—Do you need to operate dangerous machinery or drive a vehicle? Sometimes medications may interfere with concentration or cause sedation, but these effects are usually temporary.

Of special note to women—Are you pregnant or is there a possibility of pregnancy while taking medication for posttraumatic stress disorder? Are you or will you be breast-feeding your baby?

The use of medications during pregnancy and breast-feeding is a complicated issue. It is known that these medicines cross from the mother's blood to the fetus so it is important to discuss possible risks with your doctor to determine whether the particular medication you are taking should be lowered in dose or temporarily discontinued. In general, the most commonly used medications for posttraumatic stress disorder, the SSRIs, have a good safety record when taken during pregnancy.

Birth defects have occurred occasionally in babies whose mothers have taken PTSD medications during pregnancy but whether the medications actually caused the abnormalities is difficult to know (even without any exposure to medicines, a small percentage of babies will be born with malformations).

With regard to breast-feeding, all of the PTSD medications will pass into breast milk and, as a result, small amounts will get into the infant. While unlikely, it is possible that a breast-fed infant could experience mild side effects from some of these medications.

In general, to be on the safe side you should discuss with your doctor the potential risks and benefits of any medication you might be taking during pregnancy or while breast-feeding. The most conservative approach would be to avoid all medicines at these times unless the severity of the PTSD makes this impossible. Remember that exposure therapy can be an effective treatment for PTSD, and it could be an attractive alternative to medication during pregnancy and breast-feeding.

These questions are **not** comprehensive but should give you some idea of what your doctor will want to know before you begin PTSD therapy. The **main point** is to inform your doctor about **all** medical conditions, medications, etc., especially if you are being treated by several doctors. If you are not sure whether certain facts should be brought out, mention them and let your doctor decide how important they are. Without such information, a doctor would have difficulty treating you safely and effectively.

Are any laboratory tests necessary before starting medication for PTSD therapy? Laboratory tests may or may not be necessary before starting medication therapy. Depending on your medical history, age and the drug you will use, your doctor may want you to have some blood tests (often including a test of thyroid function) and an electrocardiogram (ECG or EKG).

Which PTSD medication should I start on? The choice of a specific medication is something for you and your doctor to decide, based on a number of factors. In general, SSRIs are usually tried first, followed by other antidepressants, mood stabilizers and possibly benzodiazepines. Table 2 (page 50) lists the different antidepressant medications, their usual doses, and some of their side effects. They are available only by prescription. If you tolerated and responded to a certain antidepressant in the past, the same drug would usually be the logical choice. On the other hand, drugs you did not tolerate or respond to should probably be avoided. With your help, your doctor can prescribe the medication best suited to your specific needs.

How do medications work in PTSD? The exact causes of PTSD are still unknown and so are the mechanisms of action of medications used to treat PTSD. Brain neurotransmitters (chemical messengers) such as serotonin and norepinephrine, and modulators such as neuroactive peptides (that increase or decrease the effects of neurotransmitters) are altered in PTSD. Medications that treat PTSD are thought to work by restoring a better balance of neurotransmitters and neuromodulators.

How rapidly do medications work in PTSD? On average, it takes about two weeks for an antidepressant drug to begin to work. During the first week or two side effects may be more apparent than improvement. After about two weeks side effects are usually less noticeable and PTSD symptoms begin to get weaker. Improvement is gradual and some people may not start to improve for four to six weeks. It is important not to get discouraged if you are not feeling better early in the course of the treatment. If you are discouraged, be sure to share these feelings with your doctor. Mood stabilizers usually follow a similar time course of side effects first and benefits after a few weeks.

Benzodiazepines produce their benefits and side effects quickly, often in the first few days after they are begun.

How are medications handled in the body? When taken by mouth, medications are slowly absorbed into the bloodstream and carried to all body tissues, including the brain. Most medications used to treat PTSD are gradually excreted from the body after they have been broken down (metabolized) by the liver. Since the liver is the major organ of drug metabolism, diseases or drugs affecting the liver may change drug metabolism and necessitate adjustment of dose. As people grow older, they also metabolize drugs more slowly. Lithium and gabapentin are not metabolized and are excreted unchanged in the urine.

NOTE: For the convenience of patients taking particular antidepressants, we present the following information about each class of medication in separate sections. We are aware that this may be repetitious for the general reader.

Selective serotonin reuptake inhibitors (SSRIs)

citalopram (Celexa), fluoxetine (Prozac), fluvoxamine (Luvox), paroxetine (Paxil) and sertraline (Zoloft)

General information. Serotonin is a neurotransmitter that helps transfer information from one brain cell (neuron) to another. Imbalances in serotonin are thought to play a major role in causing or continuing PTSD. Antidepressant drugs may work by correcting these imbalances. The antidepressants known as selective serotonin reuptake inhibitors (SSRIs) are unlike most other antidepressants in that they have little effect on neurotransmitters other than serotonin. Citalopram (Celexa), fluoxetine (Prozac), fluvoxamine (Luvox) (approved only for obsessive compulsive disorder in the U.S., but for depression in most countries), paroxetine (Paxil) and sertraline (Zoloft) are the SSRIs currently available in the United States. Although quite different in their chemical structures, these drugs share the property of inhibiting serotonin reuptake, so their mode of action and side effects are similar. Consequently, they will be discussed as a group.

What side effects might occur when someone is beginning SSRI therapy? During the initial adjustment period, which may last several weeks, side effects that may appear include:

More common

Decreased appetite
Nausea
Anxiety (feeling "wired")
Difficulty falling asleep
Tremor (shakiness)
Sedation
Sexual difficulties, usually delayed orgasm
Headache

Less common or rare

Blurred vision
Constipation
Diarrhea
Vomiting
Rash
Sweating

Although this list may seem long, it does not include every possible side effect. Fortunately most people experience few side effects which are usually tolerable and often decrease or disappear in a few weeks. Some may have side effects throughout treatment and a few may find the side effects intolerable.

Informing the doctor about side effects is important. Most need not be mentioned until the next scheduled appointment. However, if any are particularly distressing, cause concern or interfere with day-to-day activities, call your doctor at once.

Do I need to be on a special diet when taking an SSRI? No.

Do SSRIs cause weight gain? Unlike most other antidepressants, SSRIs are unlikely to cause weight gain. In fact, some studies show that these drugs may cause some weight loss, especially in those who are overweight prior to treatment. A few individuals may gain weight either because they lost weight because of distress and poor appetite associated with PTSD or because of an unusual reaction to the SSRI. In some people, weight gain may be a problem during long-term treatment.

May I drink alcohol while taking an SSRI? It is best to ask your doctor for a specific recommendation since there may be reasons why all alcohol should be avoided. Most people, however, may consume alcoholic beverages in **very small amounts** if they wish.

Is it dangerous to take other medications while taking an SSRI? It is best to ask your doctor for a specific recommendation. Most medications may be taken safely with SSRIs. These include pain relievers, cough and cold products, and antibiotics. Some, however, may interact with an SSRI in such a way as to cause serious side effects. For example, monoamine oxidase inhibitor (MAOI) antidepressants (isocarboxazid [Marplan], phenelzine [Nardil] and tranylcypromine [Parnate]) and the antiparkinson MAOI, selegiline (Eldepryl), should **never** be combined with SSRIs, and sufficient time must be allowed to eliminate either the MAOI or the SSRI before beginning a drug from the other class. Combining an SSRI with an MAOI may cause a "serotonin syndrome" which is characterized by confusion, sudden rise in body temperature and/or blood pressure, excessive sweating and possibly coma and death. SSRIs may inhibit the metabolism (breakdown) of certain other drugs and cause potentially dangerous increases in blood levels. The five SSRIs are not identical in this regard; therefore careful monitoring is necessary. It is best to tell **all** doctors treating you that you are taking an SSRI. Before taking **any** medication (prescription or nonprescription), ask your doctor or pharmacist whether it might interact adversely with an SSRI.

Are SSRI blood tests necessary? Tests to measure blood levels of SSRIs are not necessary.

Novel antidepressants

bupropion (Wellbutrin and Wellbutrin SR), mirtazapine (Remeron), nefazodone (Serzone), trazodone (Desyrel) and venlafaxine (Effexor and Effexor XR)

General information. Bupropion, mirtazapine, nefazodone, trazodone and venlafaxine have structures which make them different from all the other antidepressant medications and different from each other. (Mirtazapine has a tetracyclic structure but is included here because of other *novel* features.) (See Table 2, page 50.) While nefazodone and venlafaxine are recommended second line medications for PTSD, it is possible that the other novel antidepressants may also be helpful. We include them all as clinicians may prescribe them.

Bupropion has no effect on serotonin and is thought to work by correcting imbalances of norepinephrine and possibly dopamine, two other neurotransmitters. Mirtazapine has complex effects on norepinephrine and serotonin. Nefazodone and trazodone have a complex mechanism of action mainly through effects on serotonin. Venlafaxine affects both serotonin and norepinephrine, and possibly dopamine.

What side effects might occur when someone is beginning bupropion, mirtazapine, nefazodone, trazodone or venlafaxine therapy?

Bupropion: Its side effects include

Tremor (shakiness)
Restlessness
Insomnia
Dry mouth
Nausea
Headache
Dizziness
Slightly increased but low risk of seizures

Bupropion is unlikely to be sedating (restlessness and insomnia are side effects) or cause weight gain, and unlike most antidepressants, it causes little in the way of sexual dysfunction.

Mirtazapine: Its side effects include
Sedation (this "side effect" is sometimes helpful for patients suffering insomnia)
Dry mouth
Appetite increase
Weight gain
Constipation
Dizziness

Sedation and weight gain appear to be the most bothersome side effects of mirtazapine. It may cause less sexual dysfunction than many other antidepressants.

Nefazodone: Its side effects include

Sedation (this "side effect" is sometimes helpful for patients suffering insomnia)
Dry mouth
Nausea
Dizziness
Constipation
Weakness
Visual difficulties

Visual side effects are reversible and include afterimages and scotomata or spots before the eyes. Unlike many antidepressants, nefazodone causes little in the way of sexual dysfunction or weight gain.

Trazodone: Its side effects include

Sedation (this "side effect" is sometimes helpful for patients suffering insomnia)
Dry mouth
Headache
Nausea
Fainting
Dizziness
Priapism (a persistent and painful erection)

Priapism is a very rare side effect but may require emergency treatment. Nausea and faintness are more likely to occur if the drug is taken on an empty stomach.

Venlafaxine: Its side effects include

Asthenia (feelings of weakness)
Sleepiness
Sweating
Nausea
Appetite loss
Constipation
Dizziness
Nervousness
Insomnia
Increased blood pressure (uncommon)

Most people experience few, if any, side effects from these antidepressants. Those that do occur usually reflect the body's initial response to drug therapy and often disappear in a few weeks. As with any drug, some people may experience side effects with these novel antidepressants that are not included in the list.

Fortunately, side effects are not likely to be medically dangerous when the drugs are taken as prescribed. On the other hand, if an overdose is taken, the toxic effects may be quite dangerous. So, do not take more medication than prescribed in order to get a "quick" response (it won't work) or to make up for missed doses.

Informing your doctor about side effects is important. Most need not be mentioned until the next scheduled appointment. However, if any are particularly distressing, cause concern, or interfere with day-to-day activities, do not hesitate to contact the doctor at once. If you have trouble with a certain side effect, dosage adjustment or changing to a different medication should help.

It is a good idea to be cautious when operating machinery or driving until it is clear how the antidepressant medication affects mental functioning.

Do I need to be on a special diet when taking bupropion, mirtazapine, nefazodone, trazodone or venlafaxine? No.

Do bupropion, mirtazapine, nefazodone, trazodone or venlafaxine cause weight gain? Except for mirtazapine, these antidepressants are unlikely to cause weight gain. If weight gain is a problem, you should consult your doctor since either a dose adjustment or changing to a different drug may help.

May I drink alcohol while taking bupropion, mirtazapine, nefazodone, trazodone or venlafaxine? It is best to ask your doctor for a specific recommendation since there may be reasons why all alcohol should be avoided. Most people, however, may consume alcoholic beverages in **very small amounts** if they wish. However, the combination of alcohol and antidepressant medications may cause excessive sedation or drowsiness.

Is it dangerous to take other medications while taking bupropion, mirtazapine, nefazodone, trazodone or venlafaxine? It is best to ask your doctor for a specific recommendation. Most medications may be taken safely with these antidepressants. Some, however, may interact with these drugs in such a way as to cause serious side effects. Therefore, it is best to tell **all** doctors treating you that you are taking an antidepressant drug. Before taking **any** medication (prescription or nonprescription), ask your doctor or pharmacist whether it might interact adversely with the drug you are taking.

Most of the common medications such as pain relievers, cough and cold products, and antibiotics may be used safely when taking these drugs. Again, to be on the safe side, check with your doctor or pharmacist about any possible risks from combining bupropion, mirtazapine, nefazodone, trazodone or venlafaxine with other drugs. Remember—combining antidepressants with monoamine oxidase inhibitor drugs can be quite dangerous (see pages 30 and 43).

Are blood tests necessary when using bupropion, mirtazapine, nefazodone, trazodone or venlafaxine? No.

Why are two forms of bupropion and venlafaxine available? The sustained release form of bupropion (Wellbutrin SR) and the extended release form of venlafaxine (Effexor XR) both allow the drugs to enter the bloodstream more slowly and reach a lower peak blood level than the older immediate release preparations (Wellbutrin and Effexor). As a result, fewer daily doses are necessary (twice daily with Wellbutrin SR and once daily with Effexor XR) and side effects may be fewer.

Tricyclic antidepressants (TCAs)

General information. The tricyclic antidepressants were developed in the late 1950s. Imipramine was the first compound available and amitriptyline the second. While the nine tricyclics in Table 2 (page 50) share a common three-ring or "tricyclic" chemical structure, they are not identical. The composition of the rings and the chemicals attached to the rings are what make them different. Since their general chemical properties are similar, their mode of action and their side effects are somewhat alike. The tricyclics will be discussed as a group although certain differences will be pointed out.

Do tricyclics have side effects? Like all medications, tricyclics may cause side effects. It is important to recognize these side effects and know how to manage them. Some are bothersome but disappear with time; others are potentially serious, so a doctor should be consulted promptly.

What side effects might occur when someone is beginning tricyclic therapy? During the initial adjustment period, which may last several weeks, side effects that may appear include:

More common

Dry mouth
Constipation
Blurred vision
Increased heart rate
Fatigue, weakness
"Spaciness"
Muscle tremors, twitches, jitteriness
Dizziness (especially when standing up)
Sexual difficulties
Weight gain

Less common or rare
Difficulty urinating
Nausea, vomiting, heartburn
Rash
Sweating (increased or decreased)

Although this list may seem long, it does not include every possible side effect. Fortunately, most people experience a few tolerable side effects which often decrease or disappear in a few weeks. Others may experience mild to moderately severe side effects throughout therapy, and a few may find the side effects intolerable.

As you look at Table 2 (page 50), you will see that not all of the tricyclics cause the same amount of sedation, nausea or anticholinergic side effects. If you have trouble with a certain side effect, either a dose adjustment or changing to a different antidepressant may be helpful. Fortunately, these side effects are not likely to be medically dangerous when the medications are taken as prescribed. On the other hand, an overdose of these drugs can be quite dangerous. Do not take more medication than prescribed in order to get a "quick" response or to make up for missed doses. Remember, it takes time for antidepressants to work.

Informing the doctor about side effects is important. Most need not be mentioned until the next scheduled appointment. However, if any are particularly distressing, cause concern, or interfere with day-to-day activities, contact your doctor before taking more medication.

It is a good idea to be cautious when operating machinery or driving until it is clear how the TCA affects mental functioning. Lightheadedness, sleepiness or dizziness may occur when therapy is begun but often improve as the body adjusts to the medication.

Do I need to be on a special diet when taking a tricyclic? No.

How can I deal with the side effect of weight gain? In some people, TCAs may stimulate appetite or cause weight gain for other reasons. Early recognition of this side effect is important, since weight control measures such as proper diet and exercise are more likely to be effective if begun early. If weight gain is a problem, you should consult your doctor since either a dose adjustment or changing the drug may help.

May I drink alcohol while taking a tricyclic? It is best to ask your doctor for a specific recommendation. Some feel that any alcohol intake during treatment is risky while others may allow **very limited** consumption. It is important to remember that the ability to drive and to operate hazardous machinery may be dangerously impaired by the combination of alcohol and a TCA. Those who drink large amounts of alcohol may cause lower blood levels of the antidepressant which could make it less effective.

Is it dangerous to take other medications while taking a tricyclic? It is best to ask your doctor for a specific recommendation. Most medications may be taken safely with TCAs. Some, however, may interact with a TCA and cause serious side effects. Therefore, it is best to tell **all** doctors treating you that you are taking a TCA. Before taking **any** medication (prescription or nonprescription), ask your doctor or pharmacist whether it might interact adversely with the TCA.

Some drugs that may *decrease* TCA blood levels include carbamazepine (Carbatrol, Tegretol) and barbiturates. TCA blood levels may be *increased* by a number of drugs including cimetidine (Tagamet), quinidine (Cardioquin, Quinaglute), fluoxetine (Prozac), fluvoxamine (Luvox), paroxetine (Paxil), bupropion (Wellbutrin and Zyban) and, to lesser extents, citalopram (Celexa) and sertraline (Zoloft). These lists are representative but not complete.

Interactions are not limited to one drug changing the blood level of another. Drugs with similar side effects may have additive adverse effects. For example, if two drugs cause dry mouth, severe dry mouth may occur when they are combined; if two drugs lower blood pressure, fainting may result when they are used together. Most of the common medications such as pain relievers, cough and cold products, and antibiotics may be used safely when taking TCAs. Again, check with your doctor or pharmacist about any possible risks from combining TCAs with other drugs.

Are tricyclic blood tests necessary? Close monitoring of TCA blood levels is usually not necessary. There may be times, however, when knowing the tricyclic blood level may be quite useful. These include when the drug is not working or is causing troublesome side effects, if the potential for adverse drug interactions is present, in the elderly who are particularly susceptible to side effects and in situations of overdose or suspected overdose.

What preparation is needed before a tricyclic blood level test? Blood samples are usually obtained in the morning **before** the first dose of the day is taken. Before a tricyclic blood test, make sure that no doses of tricyclic antidepressant have been forgotten and that no extra doses have been taken in the last several days. This will ensure that the test is reliable. Meals can be eaten on the day of the test, since food will not interfere with the test results. If a person forgets to take the drug regularly for several days before the blood test, the doctor should be notified and the blood test rescheduled. Otherwise the result could be misleading and might lead to incorrect dosage changes.

Monoamine oxidase inhibitors (MAOIs)

General information. The monoamine oxidase inhibitors were developed in the 1950s and were the first modern drugs to be used in the treatment of depression. There are three MAOI antidepressants available in the United States. They are isocarboxazid (Marplan), phenelzine (Nardil) and tranylcypromine (Parnate) (isocarboxazid recently returned to the U.S. market after being unavailable for several years). All MAOIs are thought to work by inhibiting the enzyme, monoamine oxidase (MAO) in the brain and restoring proper neurotransmitter balance. Although there are some differences among these drugs, their actions are similar.

What side effects might occur when someone is beginning MAOI therapy? During the initial adjustment period, which may last several weeks, side effects that may appear include:

More common

Difficulty falling asleep
Headaches
Lightheadedness
Dizziness
Weight gain
Constipation

Less common

Blurred vision
Difficulty urinating
Dry mouth
Rash
Sexual difficulties
Sleepiness
Swelling of the feet
Weakness

Although this list may seem long, it does not include every possible side effect. Fortunately, most people experience few side effects, and these are usually tolerable and often decrease or disappear in a few weeks. Others may have side effects throughout treatment and a few may find the side effects intolerable.

Informing the doctor about side effects is important. Most need not be mentioned until the next scheduled appointment. However, if any are particularly distressing, cause concern, or interfere with day-to-day activities, do not hesitate to contact the doctor at once. For example, the sudden onset of severe headache may be a sign of high blood pressure.

It is a good idea to be cautious when operating machinery or driving until it is clear how the MAOI affects mental functioning. Lightheadedness or dizziness may occur when therapy is begun.

What is the "cheese reaction?" When someone taking an MAOI eats food containing high levels of tyramine (an amino acid) or similar substances, large amounts of norepinephrine may be released and cause a dangerous increase in blood pressure. While taking an MAOI and for about two weeks after stopping one, foods with high tyramine content must be avoided (see below). The relationship between MAOIs, high blood pressure and food was first described in people who ate cheese, so this reaction is sometimes called the "cheese reaction."

Do I need to be on a special diet when taking an MAOI? YES, ABSOLUTELY. Foods with high tyramine content (in some foods, dopamine or phenylethylamine is the offending agent) may cause a sudden severe rise in blood pressure (a hypertensive reaction) when consumed **even in very small amounts** while taking MAOIs.

Foods to avoid include:

Aged cheese in any form: such as cheddar, blue cheese, camembert (cottage cheese and cream cheeses are okay)
Fermented meats: sausages, salami, pepperoni
Liver (all forms)

(continued on next page)

Broad bean pods: Chinese, English, Italian (fava)
Certain beers and wines
Smoked or pickled fish
Certain yeast extracts
Powdered protein diet supplements
Soy sauce
Sauerkraut
Chocolate (in large amounts)
Yogurt
Any overripe or unfresh food

You should go over this list with your doctor periodically to be sure it remains accurate. Your doctor may prefer to use a different list with similar but not identical foods to avoid. There are many foods you may eat without any restriction including all fresh fruits, fresh meats, poultry, fresh fish and most vegetables. You should avoid large amounts of caffeine. If you are careful in following the directions about what to eat and what not to eat, there is nothing to be afraid of. If you eat a "forbidden" food once without difficulty, it doesn't mean that the next time it will be safe. The tyramine content of a particular food may vary greatly.

Most people who take MAOIs have no difficulty following the proper diet and never have problems with a hypertensive reaction. If you have any questions about your diet, consult your doctor. It is not wise to experiment.

If, after eating a certain food, you have great discomfort, headache, sweating or flushing (which may be symptoms of a hypertensive reaction) contact your doctor and go immediately to an emergency room. Some doctors give their patients a blood pressure lowering medication such as nifedipine (Procardia, Adalat) to carry with them in case a hypertensive reaction occurs. If you suspect a hypertensive reaction and medical help is not readily available, you should take this medication according to your doctor's instruction.

May I drink alcohol while taking an MAOI? Some alcoholic beverages are rich in tyramine and when consumed **even in small amounts** may cause a hypertensive crisis. Others may be consumed safely although **only in limited amounts**. Even if you don't have an adverse reaction after drinking small amounts of alcohol (the ones allowed), you may feel sleepy. Your ability to drive and to operate dangerous machinery may be impaired by the combination of alcohol and an MAOI. Be sure to discuss alcohol use with your doctor since there may be reasons why all alcohol should be avoided.

Is it dangerous to take other medications while taking an MAOI? It is best to ask your doctor for a specific recommendation about each medication. Most medications may be taken safely with MAOIs. Some, however, may interact with MAOIs and cause serious side effects. Therefore, it is best to tell **all** doctors treating you that you are taking an MAOI. Before taking **any** medication (prescription or nonprescription) ask your doctor or pharmacist whether it might interact adversely with an MAOI. **Even ordinary over-the-counter preparations or herbal "medicines" may be dangerous when combined with an MAOI.** Aspirin, acetaminophen (Tylenol and others), ibuprofen (Advil, Motrin and others) and naproxen (Aleve, Naprosyn and others) are safe when used with an MAOI. If you have any doubt, check with your doctor or pharmacist about possible risks from combining MAOIs with any other drug.

Combining an MAOI with another antidepressant can be quite dangerous (for example, see page 30) and should be avoided. (Rarely there may be occasions when certain combinations can be used safely under close, expert supervision.)

Are MAOI blood tests necessary? Blood tests to measure blood levels of an MAOI are not necessary, but blood tests to evaluate liver function, though also not necessary, may be useful from time to time.

Benzodiazepines

Benzodiazepines are sometimes used for short-term treatment of severe anxiety. They have not been shown to be effective for treating the reexperiencing and numbing and avoidance symptoms of PTSD. Ideally, benzodiazepines would not be continued long-term because they cause physical dependency when continued more than a few weeks and may be very difficult to discontinue.

Common questions about PTSD medications

How should I store PTSD medications? Keeping the current week's supply in a plastic container divided into daily compartments can help you remember to take your medication on schedule. PTSD medication not needed for the current week's use is best stored in its original prescription container away from sources of heat or moisture and out of contact with direct sunlight. Do not store PTSD medications in the bathroom medicine cabinet where heat and moisture may cause them to break down. The liquid forms of citalopram (Celexa), fluoxetine (Prozac), paroxetine (Paxil) and sertraline (Zoloft) do not have to be refrigerated. Since all PTSD medications in large amounts are potentially poisonous, they must be kept out of reach of children. Be sure to discard medicine that is outdated or not needed.

What if I am running out of medication? If you are close to running out of medication, contact your doctor immediately to arrange to get more. In order to be effective, PTSD medications must maintain a certain blood level. That's why they are not prescribed on an "as needed" basis. Also, if you plan to discontinue PTSD medications, it is not a good idea to stop abruptly. Instead, a more gradual tapering will make it easier for your body to adjust. A decision to stop treatment should be discussed with your doctor.

What if I forget a dose? Since dosage schedules vary, it is important to ask your doctor what to do if you forget a dose. Until you have done this, safe rules to follow are:

> If you are taking two or more doses a day and you've missed your regular time by three hours or less, you should take that dose when you remember it.
>
> If it is more than three hours after the dose should have been taken, just skip the forgotten dose and resume your medication at the next regularly scheduled time. Your proper blood level will soon be reached again.

If you are taking just one daily dose, take it whenever you remember it unless the missed dose is at bedtime. In that case, just resume with your regular dose the next day.

Never double up on doses of your PTSD medications to "catch up" on those you have forgotten unless your doctor instructs you to do so. Increased doses may lead to dangerously high blood levels of some medications and annoying side effects from others. A pill container with separate compartments for individual doses may be helpful to keep you on schedule.

Can I use oral contraceptives (birth control pills) while on PTSD medications? Yes. Antidepressant medications and anxiolytics do not speed up the metabolism of the hormones in birth control pills, so there should be no increased risk of birth control failure. Some mood stabilizers may speed up metabolism of birth control pills, thereby lessening their effectiveness. All combinations of medications should be discussed with your physician and/or pharmacist.

What if I need to see another doctor or have an operation? When seeing other doctors or when undergoing any medical or surgical procedure, always tell those involved that you are taking a PTSD medication. This should help ensure that the PTSD medication is managed effectively. If possible, MAOIs should be discontinued two weeks before non-emergency surgery. Even if MAOIs cannot be stopped prior to surgery, the proper choice of anesthetic and other medications can minimize the risk of problems. Do not assume that being on a PTSD medication is only important to the doctor who prescribes it.

Are PTSD medications harmful during pregnancy or breast-feeding? Please see page 25.

Can PTSD medications be used safely in people with heart or blood pressure problems? The newer antidepressants are better tolerated by people with heart disease. These include: bupropion

(Wellbutrin and Wellbutrin SR), citalopram (Celexa), fluoxetine (Prozac), fluvoxamine (Luvox), mirtazapine (Remeron), nefazodone (Serzone), paroxetine (Paxil), sertraline (Zoloft), trazodone (Desyrel) and venlafaxine (Effexor and Effexor XR). Nefazodone and trazodone can cause hypotension (low blood pressure) and venlafaxine can occasionally cause hypertension (high blood pressure) as side effects. Overall, the tricyclic antidepressants (TCAs) and monoamine oxidase inhibitors (MAOIs) can be more problematic in people with heart disease or high blood pressure. Antianxiety medications (anxiolytics) are usually well tolerated by individuals with heart disease. Mood stabilizers are also usually well tolerated by individuals with heart disease. Be sure to ask your doctor about the safety of PTSD medications if you have heart disease.

Will PTSD medications interfere with my sexual drive and orgasm? Although PTSD itself often reduces interest in sex and decreases sexual arousal, PTSD medications may sometimes have the same effect. Tricyclic antidepressants (TCAs), monoamine oxidase inhibitors (MAOIs), selective serotonin reuptake inhibitors (SSRIs) and benzodiazepines may also cause difficulty reaching orgasm in men and women and difficulty with erections in men. Sometimes these problems improve over time but dosage reduction, treatment with another medication or switching to a different PTSD medication may be necessary. Bupropion (Wellbutrin and Wellbutrin SR), nefazodone (Serzone), and possibly mirtazapine (Remeron) seem least likely to cause sexual problems.

Can I exercise while taking PTSD medications? By all means! Regular exercise is a healthy activity for people of all ages and has been shown to have antidepressant effects as well. If you are taking a tricyclic antidepressant (TCA), a monoamine oxidase inhibitor (MAOI), nefazodone (Serzone) or trazodone (Desyrel), be sure to cool down gradually after vigorous physical activity since dizziness and decreases in blood pressure may occur if you stop abruptly. Your age and whether you have other medical problems are additional factors that should be considered with regard to exercise. Clearance to start exercising should be obtained from your physician.

Are PTSD medications addictive? The antidepressant PTSD medications are not addictive and for most, the benzodiazepines are not a problem. Individuals who have become addicted to other substances, however, might also become addicted to benzodiazepines so they should be avoided by those with this problem.

How long should I take medication for PTSD? In order to prevent relapse after improvement, treatment should not be stopped as soon as a person feels better. Relapse means the return of symptoms of PTSD after a person has improved because of premature lowering of dose or discontinuation of the PTSD medication.

To decrease the possibility of relapse, "maintenance treatment" is often necessary. The Expert Consensus Guidelines recommend a length of treatment for *acute* PTSD that is 6-12 months long; for *chronic* PTSD, 12-24 months and perhaps even longer if you are still having significant symptoms. The best course of treatment for each person must be developed individually with the doctor. Keep in mind that PTSD medications should not be stopped abruptly unless they are causing intolerable side effects. Gradually tapering the dose will reduce the risk of withdrawal symptoms or an abrupt return of symptoms of PTSD.

What if the PTSD medication I am taking does not work? A person who does not respond to one PTSD medication may very well respond to a different one. Before switching, it is important to be sure that the dose and duration of treatment have been adequate. If individual PTSD medications are ineffective, combinations of PTSD medications or adding a "booster" drug to the PTSD medication may be necessary. Although combining PTSD medications can be quite beneficial, certain combinations can be dangerous and even lethal (such as the combination of an MAOI and an SSRI or tricyclic antidepressant; see pages 30 and 43). Combining PTSD medications should be done only under close supervision by a physician experienced in their use. If you are considering using more than one PTSD medication at the same time, ask your doctor—do not try to find out yourself. This is also true for herbal remedies such as St. John's Wort.

Sometimes, instead of combining different PTSD medications, other drugs such as buspirone (BuSpar), carbamazepine (Carbatrol, Tegretol), gabapentin (Neurontin), lamotrigine (Lamictal), lithium (Eskalith, Lithobid and others), topiramate (Topamax), or valproate (Depakote, Depakene), may be added to your PTSD medication. This procedure, called augmentation, is often helpful in overcoming resistant PTSD. Importantly, an effective psychotherapy (exposure, anxiety management and cognitive therapy) may be helpful even when medications are not. The Expert Consensus Guidelines emphasized the importance of these psychotherapies with and without medications.

Are there any new drugs for treating PTSD? The search for new drugs for PTSD is an ongoing process throughout the world. Some are already available in other countries and may become available in the United States in the future. Others are currently under investigational study in this country and some of them are close to being marketed. Before the Food and Drug Administration (FDA) will approve a drug for marketing in this country, convincing evidence must be presented that it is both safe and effective. The future holds great promise for a continuing supply of new and different drugs for PTSD.

Table 2 – Antidepressant Medications

Generic Name	Brand Name in U.S.	Usual Starting Daily Dose*	Usual Effective Daily Dose*	-Side Effects- Sedation	Anticholinergic Effects**	Nausea
Selective serotonin reuptake inhibitors (SSRIs)						
Citalopram	Celexa	20	20-60	l	l	m
Fluoxetine	Prozac	20	20-80	l	l	m
Fluvoxamine***	Luvox	50	100-300	l	l	m
Paroxetine	Paxil	20	20-50	l	l	m
Sertraline†	Zoloft	50	50-200	l	l	m
Tricyclics (TCAs)						
Amitriptyline	Elavil	50-75	100-300	vh	vh	l
Amoxapine	Asendin	100-150	200-400	m	m	l
Clomipramine***	Anafranil	25	100-250	m	h	l
Desipramine	Norpramin	50	100-300	l	m	l
Doxepin	Adapin Sinequan	50-75	100-300	vh	h	l
Imipramine	Tofranil	50-75	100-300	h	h	l
Nortriptyline	Pamelor	25-50	50-150	m	m	l
Protriptyline	Vivactil	15	15-60	l	vh	l
Trimipramine	Surmontil	50-75	100-300	vh	h	l
Tetracyclic						
Maprotiline	Ludiomil	50-75	100-225	vh	m	l
Mirtazapine	Remeron	15	15-45	h	l	l
Novel						
Bupropion	Wellbutrin	200	300-450	l	l	m
	Wellbutrin SR	150	300-400	l	l	m
Nefazodone	Serzone	200	300-600	m	l	m
Trazodone	Desyrel	150	150-400	vh	l	m
Venlafaxine	Effexor	75	75-375	l	l	m
	Effexor XR	75	75-375	l	l	m
Monoamine oxidase inhibitors (MAOIs)						
Isocarboxazid	Marplan	30	30	l	l	l
Phenelzine	Nardil	30	45-90	l	l	l
Tranylcypromine	Parnate	20	30-60	l	l	l

*Lower doses are often used in elderly or medically ill patients.

**dry mouth, blurred vision, constipation, difficulty urinating, impaired memory

***While approved in the U.S. only for treating obsessive compulsive disorder, clomipramine and fluvoxamine are also effective antidepressants.

†FDA approved for PTSD

Side effect severity: l = low; m = medium; h = high; vh = very high

How can someone learn all that is important about PTSD and its treatments?

A booklet of this size cannot provide answers to every question that might be asked about PTSD. The material included here was selected because doctors and those being treated for PTSD felt it was especially important.

The following suggestions may help people learn more about PTSD and its treatments:

- Read this booklet thoroughly, making sure to note any areas where you may have questions.
- Ask your doctor these questions and any others you might have.
- Re-read this booklet from time to time to refresh your memory. Share it with close friends and family members and discuss areas that are particularly important to you.
- Refer to the readings suggested on the following pages.
- Self-help groups are forming in different parts of the country to offer support and information to people with PTSD. There may be such a group in your community. An excellent source of information about individuals with knowledge about treating PTSD is the **Madison Institute of Medicine** website on PTSD at www.ptsd.factsforhealth.org. The Madison Institute of Medicine Information Centers have patient guides on many psychiatric disorders (see page 69), and the world's most comprehensive registries of publications on bipolar and obsessive compulsive disorders (for address, see page 66). Their website is www.miminc.org. The **Anxiety Disorders Association of America (ADAA)** offers support and information. The address is 11900 Parklawn Drive, Suite 100, Rockville, MD 20852-2624, (301) 231-9350. Their website is www.adaa.org.

Summary and Conclusions

Unfortunately, exposure to extreme trauma is fairly common. For those exposed to extreme trauma, acute posttraumatic stress disorder can occur and, for a smaller proportion, the disorder lasts more than 3 months and becomes chronic PTSD. Although chronic PTSD sufferers tend to improve with the passage of time, their progress can be substantially accelerated with presently available psychotherapies and medications. Psychotherapies will require work on the part of the patient and sometimes willingness to tolerate some short-term increase in discomfort in order to obtain long-term relief of suffering and improvement in functioning. Medications, too, may cause side effects, most of which will be mild and diminish as one gets used to the medication or as dose is adjusted to optimize treatment response.

Posttraumatic stress disorder is very difficult for those who experience it and for their families, friends and coworkers. We are fortunate to have treatments that alleviate suffering for many of those with PTSD. While some discomfort may remain, improvements are usually quite worthwhile and gratifying. As new knowledge about PTSD emerges, you can find it reviewed and updated on **www.ptsd.factsforhealth.org**.

Suggested Readings

The following publications may be helpful in better understanding posttraumatic stress disorder and its treatment. They can be obtained through bookstores and libraries.

Nontechnical

Children Changed by Trauma. Alexander DW. New Harbinger Publications, Oakland, CA, 1999

Coping With Trauma: A Guide to Self Understanding. Allen JG. American Psychiatric Press, Washington, DC, 1995

Feeling Good: The New Mood Therapy. Burns DD. Avon Books, New York, rev. ed., 1999

Rebuilding Shattered Lives: The Rational and Responsible Treatment of Post-Traumatic and Dissociative Disorders. Chu JA. John Wiley & Sons, New York, 1998

Reclaiming Your Life After Rape: A Cognitive-Behavioral Therapy for PTSD. Rothbaum BO, Foa EB. Psychological Corporation, San Antonio, TX, 1999

The Scared Child: Helping Kids Overcome Traumatic Events. Brooks B, Siegel PM. John Wiley & Sons, New York, 1996

Trauma and Recovery. Herman JL. BasicBooks, New York, 1997

Trust After Trauma: A Guide to Relationships for Survivors and Those Who Love Them. Matsakis A. New Harbinger Publications, Oakland, CA, 1998

Your Mental Health. Frances A, First MB. Scribner, New York, 1998

Technical

Aging and Posttraumatic Stress Disorder. Ruskin PE, Talbott JA (eds). American Psychiatric Press, Washington, DC, 1996

Diagnostic and Statistical Manual of Mental Disorders, Fourth Edition. American Psychiatric Association, Washington, DC, 1994

Essential Papers on Posttraumatic Stress Disorder. Horowitz MJ (ed). New York University Press, New York, 1999

Expert Consensus Guideline Series: Treatment of Posttraumatic Stress Disorder. Expert Consensus Panels for PTSD. *Journal of Clinical Psychiatry* 60(Suppl 16), 1999

Posttraumatic Stress Disorder: Acute and Long-Term Response to Trauma and Disaster. Fullerton CS, Ursano RJ (eds). American Psychiatric Press, Washington, DC, 1997

Posttraumatic Stress Disorder: A Clinical Review. Pynoos RS (ed). Sidran Press, Lutherville, MD, 1994

Posttraumatic Stress Disorder: A Comprehensive Text. Saigh PA, Bremner JD (eds). Allyn & Bacon, Boston, 2nd ed., 1998

Posttraumatic Stress Disorder: DSM-IV and Beyond. Davidson JRT, Foa EB (eds). American Psychiatric Press, Washington, DC, 1993

Post-Traumatic Stress Disorder in Children. Eth S, Pynoos RS (eds). American Psychiatric Press, Washington, DC, 1985

Psychobiology of Posttraumatic Stress Disorder. (Annals of the New York Academy of Sciences, Volume 821). Yehuda R, McFarlane AC (eds). New York Academy of Sciences, New York, 1997

Psychological Assessment of Adult Posttraumatic States. Briere J. American Psychological Association, Washington, DC, 1997

Risk Factors for Posttraumatic Stress Disorder. Yehuda R (ed). American Psychiatric Press, Washington, DC, 1999

Treating the Trauma of Rape: Cognitive-Behavioral Therapy for PTSD. Foa EB, Rothbaum BO (eds). Guilford Publications, New York, 1997

Resources

In addition to the Madison Institute of Medicine PTSD web site: **www.ptsd.factsforhealth.org** (see pages 51 and 52), the following organizations can be contacted for information and support:

Anxiety Disorders Association of America (ADAA)
11900 Parklawn Drive, Suite 100
Rockville, MD 20852-2624
301-231-9350
Web site: www.adaa.org

International Society for Traumatic Stress Studies (ISTSS)
60 Revere Drive, Suite 500
Northbrook, IL 60062
847-480-9028
Web site: www.istss.org

National Alliance for the Mentally Ill (NAMI)
Colonial Place Three
2107 Wilson Blvd, Suite 300
Arlington, VA 22201-3042
800-950-NAMI (800-950-6264)
Web site: www.nami.org

National Depressive and Manic-Depressive Association (NDMDA)
730 N. Franklin St., Suite 501
Chicago, IL 60610-3526
800-82-NDMDA (800-826-3632)
Web site: www.ndmda.org

National Mental Health Association (NMHA)
National Mental Health Information Center
1021 Prince Street
Alexandria, VA 22314-2971
800-969-NMHA (800-969-6642)
Web site: www.nmha.org

National Organization for Victim Assistance (NOVA)
1757 Park Road, NW
Washington, DC 20010
202-232-6682
Web site: www.try-nova.org

National Victim Center
2111 Wilson Boulevard, Suite 300
Arlington, VA 22201
800-394-2255
Web site: www.nvc.org

Appendix

Diagnostic criteria for Posttraumatic Stress Disorder from the *Diagnostic and Statistical Manual of Mental Disorders, Fourth Edition*

A. The person has been exposed to a traumatic event in which both of the following were present:

   (1) the person experienced, witnessed, or was confronted with an event or events that involved actual or threatened death or serious injury, or a threat to the physical integrity of self or others

   (2) the person's response involved intense fear, helplessness, or horror.
   Note: In children, this may be expressed instead by disorganized or agitated behavior

B. The traumatic event is persistently reexperienced in one (or more) of the following ways:

   (1) recurrent and intrusive distressing recollections of the event, including images, thoughts, or perceptions. **Note:** In young children, repetitive play may occur in which themes or aspects of the trauma are expressed.

   (2) recurrent distressing dreams of the event. **Note:** In children, there may be frightening dreams without recognizable content.

   (3) acting or feeling as if the traumatic event were recurring (includes a sense of reliving the experience, illusions, hallucinations, and dissociative flashback episodes, including those that occur on awakening or when intoxicated). **Note:** In young children, trauma-specific reenactment may occur.

   (4) intense psychological distress at exposure to internal or external cues that symbolize or resemble an aspect of the traumatic event

   (5) physiological reactivity on exposure to internal or external cues that symbolize or resemble an aspect of the traumatic event

C. Persistent avoidance of stimuli associated with the trauma and numbing of general responsiveness (not present before the trauma), as indicated by three (or more) of the following:

(1) efforts to avoid thoughts, feelings, or conversations associated with the trauma
(2) efforts to avoid activities, places, or people that arouse recollections of the trauma
(3) inability to recall an important aspect of the trauma
(4) markedly diminished interest or participation in significant activities
(5) feeling of detachment or estrangement from others
(6) restricted range of affect (e.g., unable to have loving feelings)
(7) sense of a foreshortened future (e.g., does not expect to have a career, marriage, children, or a normal life span)

D. Persistent symptoms of increased arousal (not present before the trauma), as indicated by two (or more) of the following:

(1) difficulty falling or staying asleep
(2) irritability or outbursts of anger
(3) difficulty concentrating
(4) hypervigilance
(5) exaggerated startle response

E. Duration of the disturbance (symptoms in Criteria B, C, and D) is more than 1 month.

F. The disturbance causes clinically significant distress or impairment in social, occupational, or other important areas of functioning.

Specify if:

Acute: if duration of symptoms is less than 3 months
Chronic: if duration of symptoms is 3 months or more

Specify if:

With Delayed Onset: if onset of symptoms is at least 6 months after the stressor

Glossary

Addiction: Addiction means psychological and physical dependence on a substance that requires the individual to use more and more of the substance in order to obtain the same effect. Because withdrawal of addictive substances is often distressing and sometimes dangerous, it is difficult for individuals who are addicted to stop using the addictive substance. Many organize their lives around their addiction and may have to steal in order to purchase their addictive substance through illicit channels where it is available. Please note: physical dependence by itself is *not* addiction. Many of us are physically dependent on our eye glasses but this functional physical dependence improves our performance in contrast to the dysfunctional physical dependence that occurs in addiction.

Adjunctive treatment: Treatment added to the main treatment (see also **Augmentation**).

Anticholinergic: The cholinergic nerve fibers release acetylcholine. Some medications block the effects of acetylcholine and may cause anticholinergic side effects such as dry mouth, constipation, blurred vision and occasionally, difficulty urinating or thinking clearly.

Arousal: When asleep, we have a very low level of arousal. In fact, when we wake up, we are said to be aroused. Arousal increases and declines throughout the day in response to our need to be alert. Extreme arousal is usually unpleasant, often interferes with functioning, and we try to change our circumstances to achieve a more positive and comfortable level of arousal. Those with PTSD are more aroused than necessary for safety, and this hyperarousal interferes with their comfort, functioning, and ability to relax and fall asleep.

Augmentation (Add-on): The addition of a second (or sometimes a third and fourth) medication to the first medication used to treat a disorder. In treating hypertension (high blood pressure), asthma, diabetes, depression and many other disorders, physicians often employ more than one medication. For PTSD, physicians might prescribe an SSRI as the primary medication and add a benzodiazepine to improve sleep if the SSRI alone produced insufficient improvement in sleep. In the past, combining medications was considered a negative practice and labeled polypharmacy. We now recognize that many disorders including PTSD may require augmentation therapy. As William Osler, a highly respected physician said, "The true polypharmacy is the skillful combination of remedies."

Avoidance: We all avoid things that are unpleasant and especially things that are dangerous. That's understandable. Those with PTSD may avoid things that are not considered by most people to be unusually unpleasant or dangerous. This inappropriate avoidance occurs through a process called generalization, where a neutral object or situation becomes charged with new meaning. For example, a person assaulted in a dark doorway may worry about and avoid all doorways, even those that are brightly lit and staffed by a doorman.

Diagnostic criteria: Diagnoses are based on symptoms patients describe, signs physicians find on physical examination and results of laboratory evaluations. Diagnostic criteria are sometimes present and sometimes absent and specific numbers of criteria are usually required to make a particular diagnosis. Criteria for PTSD are found in the Appendix (pages 57-58) and a checklist of criteria begins on page 5.

ECG or EKG: Abbreviations for electrocardiogram. See definition on page 61.

Efficacy: Efficacy, to those who delve into such details, means how well treatment works in a controlled research study. *Effectiveness* describes how well a treatment works in routine care. For most purposes, the terms are interchangeable.

Electrocardiogram: A test of the heart's electrical activity. Electrodes are attached to each arm and leg (usually with wide rubber bands) and across the left chest. The electrodes are connected to an electrocardiograph through insulated wires. Electrocardiograms show heart rate and rhythm.

EMDR: The abbreviation for eye movement desensitization reprocessing. See definition below.

Emotional numbing: We've all had an arm go numb when we've slept in a funny position. In PTSD, emotional numbing can develop to experiences that were previously pleasurable. It's as though the person's emotional responses are turned down as a way of protecting against reexperiencing the trauma. Sometimes this is called emotional anesthesia.

Exposure: Exposure therapy involves facing triggers of anxiety and then remaining in contact with the triggers until anxiety dampens down. This predictable decrease in anxiety is called habituation (see definition below).

Eye movement desensitization reprocessing: A form of exposure therapy in which an individual is asked to hold a traumatic event in their consciousness while moving their eyes in a particular manner. Not rated highly by the Expert Consensus Panels for treatment of PTSD.

Flashbacks: The sensation, while awake, that a past experience is happening again. Flashbacks can be positive, neutral or negative. PTSD flashbacks are always negative and upsetting.

Habituation: The act of making habitual or customary. A decrease in responsiveness upon repeated exposure to a stimulus. The process of getting used to annoying memories of past traumatic experiences so that they no longer have a negative effect.

Hyperventilation: Hyper (excessive) ventilation (breathing). Hyperventilation can take the form of breathing too rapidly or too deeply or both. Normal breathing at rest occurs 12 to 15 times per minute or once every 4 to 5 seconds. When we are active, our breathing rate increases and when we're very active, it can increase a lot, even to 60 or more times a minute. But if we breathe faster than needed to meet our body's current need for exchange of oxygen and carbon dioxide, that is hyperventilation. When we hyperventilate, we exhale too much carbon dioxide and the imbalances that result can cause distressing though not dangerous symptoms, including lightheadedness, dizziness, feeling faint, and numbness and tingling sensations called paresthesias.

Hypervigilance: A state of being more alert than usual. Individuals with PTSD who are hypervigilant are more alert in general and are particularly watching for things associated with the traumatic experience.

In vivo exposure: Real life exposure therapy as contrasted with exposure in the imagination. Imaginal exposure is less frightening than in vivo exposure; it is also less effective.

Indication: A treatment indication means that the treatment is recognized as safe and clearly beneficial for a disorder. The U.S. Food and Drug Administration (FDA) gives approvals for labeling a medication as effective for a particular disorder after weighing all research on the risks and benefits. The first FDA indication for PTSD was for sertraline (Zoloft), an SSRI.

MAOI: Abbreviation for monoamine oxidase inhibitor. See definition below.

Monoamine oxidase inhibitors: This class of medications is thought to work by inhibiting the enzyme monoamine oxidase in the brain and restoring proper neurotransmitter balance. The monoamine oxidase inhibitors are listed on page 40.

Neuroactive peptides: Molecules made up of short chains of amino acids (endorphins, enkephalins, vasopressin, etc.) that are found in the brain, often in the synapses which are small spaces between nerve endings where chemical activity occurs.

Neuromodulators: Neuromodulators increase or decrease (modulate) the effects of neurotransmitters. Neuromodulators are also released by nerves and convey information to nearby or distant nerves, either enhancing or damping their activities. Neuropeptides are often neuromodulators.

Neurotransmitters: These brain messengers are chemicals that accomplish electrochemical reactions between nerve endings. The main neurotransmitters involved in the central nervous system are serotonin (5-HT), norepinephrine (NE), dopamine (DA), gamma-aminobutyric acid (GABA), acetylcholine (ACh) and glutamate (GLU).

Novel: New, unusual or different.

Off-label: The FDA permits labeling of medications for treating specific disorders if the medication has shown clear benefit and tolerable risks (see **Indication**). The process of achieving an FDA approved indication is long and very costly. Many medications that work for a disorder have not obtained FDA approval to be labeled for that disorder. Physicians may still prescribe them, and this practice is called off-label prescribing.

Psychopharmacology: The study of medication effects on the psyche or mind. Psychopharmacologists use medications to treat medical or psychiatric disorders that affect thoughts, feelings and behaviors.

Relapse: Worsening of a disorder after some improvement or recovery has occurred. If the person has recovered completely from the disorder only recently, many clinicians will describe that worsening as a relapse rather than a recurrence, although the amount of time that must pass before a relapse would be called a recurrence is arbitrary.

Sedation: Feeling of being sleepy brought on by medication or other substances such as alcohol.

Selective serotonin reuptake inhibitors: Sometimes the first two words are reversed (serotonin selective reuptake inhibitors). This class of medications inhibits or reduces the reuptake of serotonin into nerve cells or neurons. Since they inhibit the reuptake of only serotonin, they are called selective, to differentiate them from other medications that inhibit reuptake of more than one neurotransmitter. Selectivity is relative—when serotonin levels change, levels of other neurotransmitters and neuromodulators often change too. These medications are discussed on pages 28-30.

Sexual dysfunction: Interference with interest in sex, sexual arousal and ability to achieve orgasm. Medications sometimes cause sexual dysfunction, most often delaying or preventing orgasm.

SSRI: The abbreviation for selective serotonin reuptake inhibitor. See definition above.

Startle response or reaction: All human beings can be startled by unexpected sights, sounds and contact. This normal response is protective. People with PTSD may startle at things that are not normally alarming to the point that their exaggerated startle response becomes wearing.

Stimuli: Anything that affects the mind or body. An unexpected pin-prick is a stimulus that leads one to pull away from it.

TCA: The abbreviation for tricyclic antidepressant. See definition on page 65.

Tolerability: How easy it is for a treatment to be taken. All medications cause side effects in some people. If the side effects are mild enough, the patient can keep taking the medicine—it is tolerable.

Tremor: Shaking. Usually noted in outstretched fingers or hands but sometimes identifiable as head bobbing. Mild tremors may be overlooked, while more marked tremors are easily noticed.

Tricyclic antidepressants: A chemical group of antidepressant medications that share a three-ringed nucleus. Since their general chemical properties are similar, their mode of action and side effects are somewhat alike. They are discussed as a group beginning on page 36, although their differences are pointed out.

We hope to revise and update this booklet from time to time. Your comments, suggestions and criticisms are most welcome. To share your ideas or to order additional booklets, please contact:

Information Centers
Madison Institute of Medicine, Inc.
7617 Mineral Point Road, Suite 300
Madison, WI 53717
Telephone (608) 827-2470
Fax (608) 827-2479
E-mail: mim@healthtechsys.com
www.miminc.org

The Madison Institute of Medicine is a nonprofit organization. Its Information Centers are dependent, in part, on user fees and contributions for support.

PRICES *(Subject to change)*	
1-9 copies	$5.95 each
10-49 copies	$3.95 each
50 or more copies	$2.50 each
SHIPPING AND HANDLING CHARGES	
If your order totals	*Add*
Up to $5.99	$ 2.00
$6.00 - $35.99	$ 4.00
$36.00 - $149.99	$ 6.00
$150.00 and up	$10.00

FOR ORDERS SHIPPED OUTSIDE THE U.S. CONTACT THE INFORMATION CENTERS FOR POSTAGE CHARGES.

PLEASE MAKE CHECKS PAYABLE TO MADISON INSTITUTE OF MEDICINE.

Notes and Questions

Notes and Questions